Based on a true story.

In memory of my Granny

Text 2024 Copyright Woolwine Dunn LLC
All rights reserved. No part of this book may be reproduced in any form without the express written permission from the author and publisher, except as permitted by U.S. copyright law. For permission requests, send an email to the publisher addressed "Attention: Lisa Dunn" at the email address below.

Published by Woolwine Dunn LLC
Owner, Lisa Dunn
lisawdunn@gmail.com

Written and illustrated by Lisa Dunn

Edited by Michael J. via Reedsy.com

Printed in the United States of America

First printing 2024

ISBN 979-8-9920411-0-1

# Glass from the Sea

Written and Illustrated by
Lisa Dunn

My Granny lived in a beach house. I loved visiting her. She had a beautiful blue-green colored vase. It sat on a small, old table that wobbled when it was barely touched. I had to be super-duper careful when I walked by it so I wouldn't knock it over and break that beautiful vase.

On one of my visits to Granny's house, I was playing with my doll near that rickety old table. I forgot to be careful and bumped right into it. It fell over... and so did that beautiful blue-green colored vase. It shattered into what felt like a million pieces.

I couldn't believe what I just did. I started to cry, and my whole body began shaking. My heart was beating really fast too. I got scared because I broke something that both Granny and I loved. My crying got louder and louder.

Granny heard the crash and my crying and ran into the room to check on me. "Is everything alright? Did you get hurt?" she asked.

Between sobs, I told her how I forgot to be careful, and I made the table fall and the vase broke.

Granny hugged me tight and said accidents happen to everyone, and that she was so glad that I didn't get cut by the broken glass. "I'm so sorry Granny, please don't be mad at me," I said.

"Sweetheart," Granny said, "it was just a decoration. You are more important than that silly vase. There are going to be times in our lives when things go wrong and accidents will happen, even to me. But what matters is that we learn from them and do our best to be more careful next time." She kissed my cheek and handed me a tissue.

Once I wiped my tears away, I looked at the mess on the floor. I thought the scattered glass all over the floor was just as beautiful as the vase had been. There were large pieces, small pieces, and even teeny tiny little pieces.

When the sunlight hit them just right, they sparkled and shined. I was still sad that I broke the vase, but seeing how the remnants twinkled and glistened, I was in love!

Granny swept up all the broken fragments and tossed them into the trash. It made me sad to see something so beautiful get thrown away, but Granny said it was to protect me from cuts.

Granny saw that I was still upset about it, and she didn't like to see me that way. "Come sit by me and let me tell you a story," she said.

"I can see how much you love the pieces of shiny broken glass." Granny said, "And you know what? I love them, too. But now is not the right time to try and hold on to them. If you were to grab any of those pieces, they could cut you.

But you'd never believe what happens to those pieces of glass once they get to the trash dump. It's something incredibly magical."

"You know, sometimes birds like to pick up twigs, sticks, and leaves to use when building their nests. Sometimes they pick up odd things that you wouldn't expect they would use, like plastic, paper, or even glass. And sometimes when they pick up a piece of glass, it falls out of their beaks and lands in the water. If the piece is large enough, it will sink right down to the bottom to sit in the sand. The smaller pieces will float along with the waves of water."

Granny paused and looked off into the distance. When she stopped talking, I looked up and saw her smiling. It made me smile, too. She must be imagining how a piece of her vase might get dropped in the water and rolled around on one of those big waves before it washes up on the shore. Granny leaned in a bit closer to me.

"The secret to broken glass becoming sea glass is one of my favorite parts. While the glass is in the water, it moves around so much that it gets tossed about with the waves and currents, bumped against rocks and shells, and the salt and sand in the water rub against it, smoothing out the sharp edges. It takes a long time for that magic to happen—but when it does happen—it creates something beautiful out of something that was broken."

I asked Granny how she knew about that stuff.

"Well," Granny said, "I love them so much that I did a little research about it because I have found some amazing pieces of smoothed edged glass. They are different sizes, shapes, and colors, too. Would you like to see them?"

"YES!" I said, "I would LOVE to."

"Come with me, love," Granny said. I followed her into her bedroom, where she took a glass jar off a shelf. It was filled with pieces of beautiful sea glass. "Would you like to hold them?" I nodded. She poured some pieces into my hand. "Feel how smooth the edges are," she said.

I slowly turned one over and over with my fingers, inspecting every side of it and tracing the edges. They look like they would be rough, but Granny said the elements have made them appear to be frosted.

"Frosted glass lets light shine through, but you can't really see through it. Just like the glass on my shower door. Do you understand what I mean?" I nodded my head and asked, "Granny, can you help me find some to take home with me? I want to put them in a jar just like you have." Granny smiled. "Put your shoes on, my love. Let's take a walk along the beach and look for sea glass."

Granny and I walked along the shore of the beach. She told me to look for something that was a different color than the usual shells I saw. "Sometimes the glass is the same color as the shells," Granny said. "But if you look closely, the shells have different colors on each one. The glass piece will usually just have one color. You can find brown, blue, green, white, clear, and sometimes purple glass pieces."

We continued to walk along the beach for a little while longer. It wasn't very long before I found my first piece of glass. It was small and brown. Granny said it may have been an old soda bottle from when she was a little girl. Imagining that was so exciting to me...

...it was my very first piece of sea glass.

When I got home, I asked my mommy for a jar to put them in. My sea glass sat in a jar on a shelf in my bedroom...

## Author's Note

Now that I am all grown up, I never stop looking for sea glass. Every beach trip my family and I take—whether it's to Galveston, Texas or Honolulu, Hawaii—I still search for sea glass. I bring home what I find, clean the sand off, and place them in jars all around my house. I still love the shiny and sparkly, large and small, smooth-edged pieces of sea glass. And because I love it so much, I taught my own children how to find sea glass. My daughters fell in love with finding them, and they, too, have jars of sea glass in their homes that they found. Please don't mistake this hobby as stealing from beaches. Taking sand and shells from some beaches is illegal (which means it's against the law). However, picking up sea glass from beaches is a helpful way to do your part to keep the beaches clean and is encouraged. Enjoy your search.

www.ingramcontent.com/pod-product-compliance
Lightning Source LLC
LaVergne TN
LVHW062001070526
838199LV00060B/4234